Pebble®
Plus

Physical Science

Sound

by Abbie Dunne

raintree

a Capstone company — publishers for children

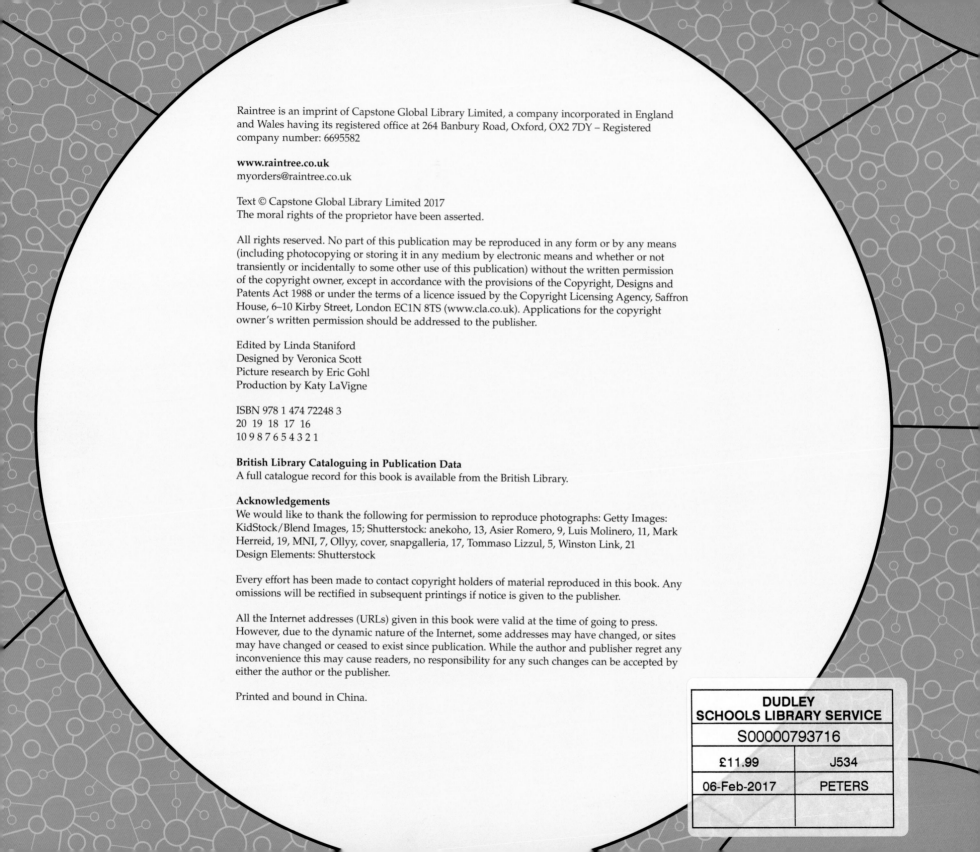

Raintree is an imprint of Capstone Global Library Limited, a company incorporated in England and Wales having its registered office at 264 Banbury Road, Oxford, OX2 7DY – Registered company number: 6695582

www.raintree.co.uk
myorders@raintree.co.uk

Edited by Linda Staniford
Designed by Veronica Scott
Picture research by Eric Gohl
Production by Katy LaVigne

ISBN 978 1 474 72248 3
20 19 18 17 16
10 9 8 7 6 5 4 3 2 1

British Library Cataloguing in Publication Data
A full catalogue record for this book is available from the British Library.

Acknowledgements
We would like to thank the following for permission to reproduce photographs: Getty Images: KidStock/Blend Images, 15; Shutterstock: anekoho, 13, Asier Romero, 9, Luis Molinero, 11, Mark Herreid, 19, MNI, 7, Ollyy, cover, snapgalleria, 17, Tommaso Lizzul, 5, Winston Link, 21
Design Elements: Shutterstock

Every effort has been made to contact copyright holders of material reproduced in this book. Any omissions will be rectified in subsequent printings if notice is given to the publisher.

All the Internet addresses (URLs) given in this book were valid at the time of going to press. However, due to the dynamic nature of the Internet, some addresses may have changed, or sites may have changed or ceased to exist since publication. While the author and publisher regret any inconvenience this may cause readers, no responsibility for any such changes can be accepted by either the author or the publisher.

Printed and bound in China.

Contents

What is sound?

Sound is made up of waves.
Sound waves are made
when something vibrates.
The vibrating object sends
waves into the air.

The vibrations move through air

like ripples on a pond.

This is how sound waves spread.

We can't see sound waves,

but we can hear them.

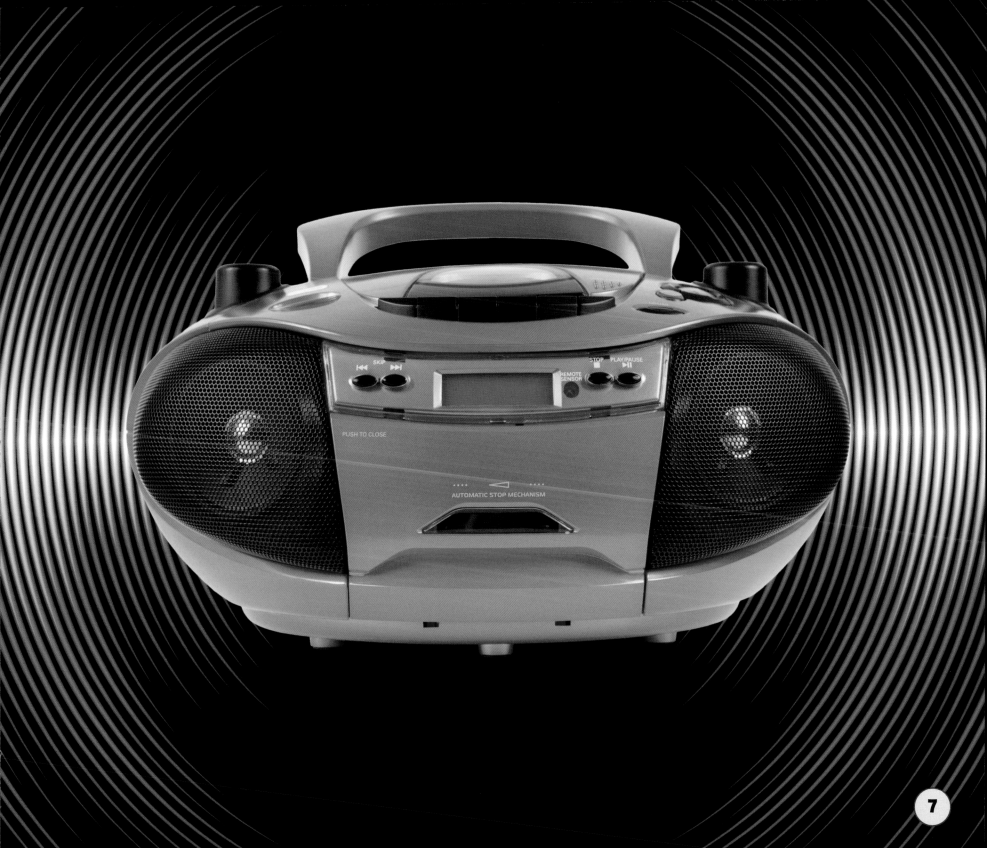

How do sound waves travel?

Sound waves spread out in all directions. They bounce back if they hit something solid, such as a wall. The waves stop if they hit something that absorbs them.

Loud noises travel farther.
A megaphone makes the
human voice louder.
It makes the sound waves
travel in the same direction.

Megaphone

Making sounds

There are many ways
to make sounds. You can
tap, rub or scrape one object
against another. Machines make
noises as their parts move.

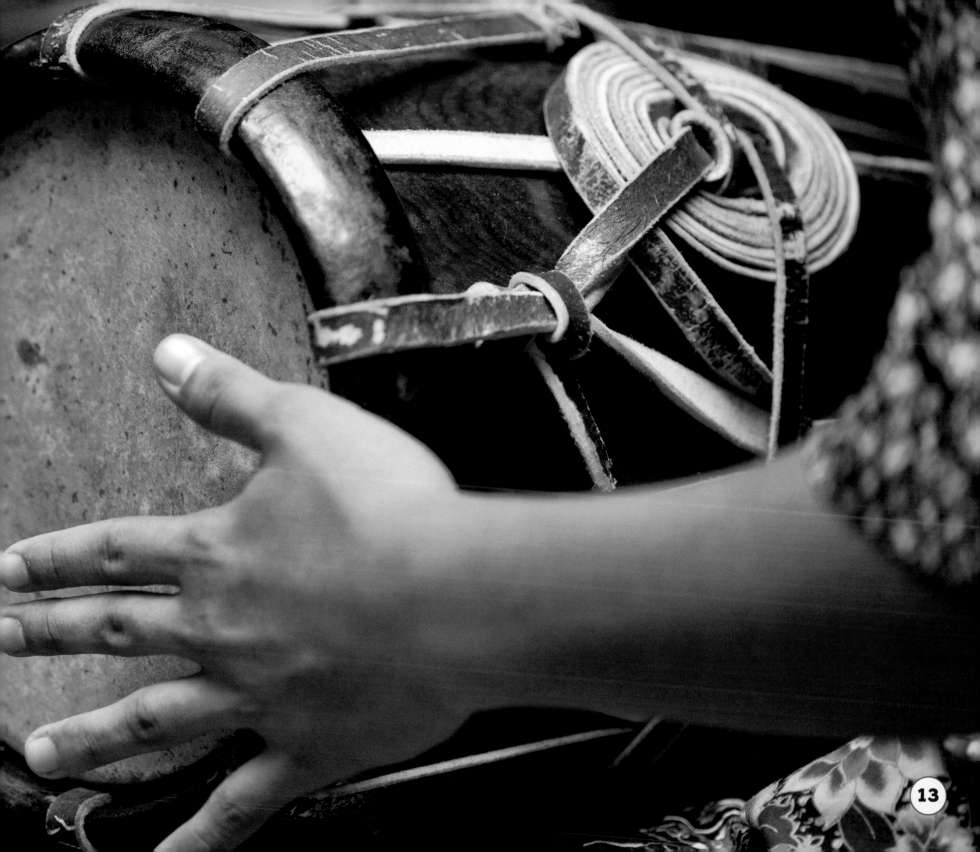

Different musical instruments make different sounds. Some are blown. Others are struck. Some have strings that are plucked or scraped.

How we hear sound

Your ear catches sound waves.

The waves move inside

your ear. The sound waves

make your eardrum vibrate.

A nerve sends sound to the brain.

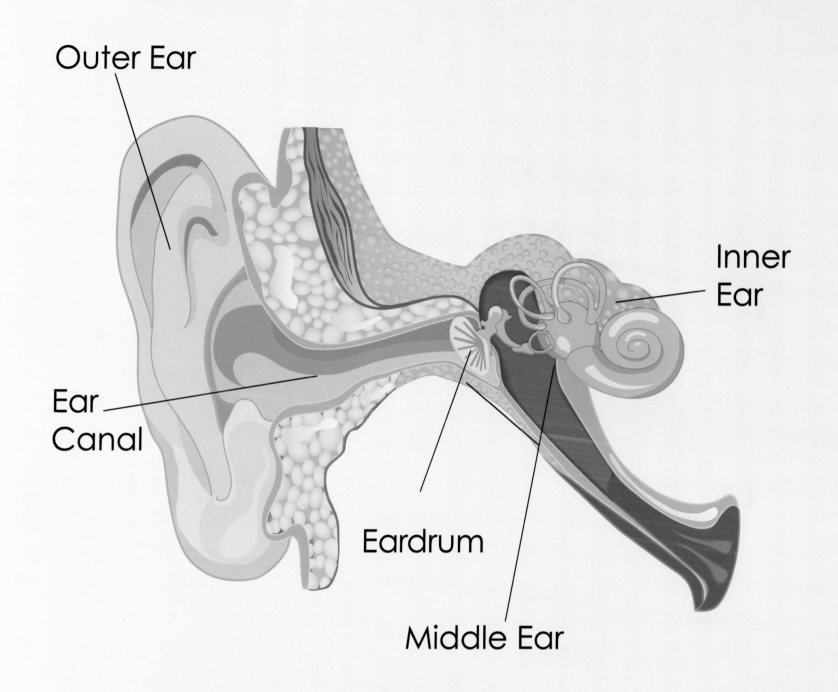

Outer Ear

Inner Ear

Ear Canal

Eardrum

Middle Ear

17

Pitch is how high or low a sound is. The sound made by a big drum has a low pitch. The sound made by a tiny bell has a high pitch.

19

Activity

Investigating vibrations and sound

How can you show that vibrations make sound and that sound makes things vibrate? Follow the steps below to find out.

What you need

- drum, or a drum made by stretching a balloon across the top of a lidless can

- 2 pencils or drumsticks

- paper

- grains of rice

What you do

1. Beat the drum with the pencils or drumsticks.

2. Make notes about what you hear and see.

3. Now place the grains of rice on the drum. Beat the drum with the pencils again.

4. Make notes about what you hear and see.

What do you think?

Make claims.

Claims are things you believe to be true. How did you show that vibrations make sound and that sound makes things vibrate?

Use what you saw while beating the drum with and without the rice to support your claims.

Glossary

eardrum   thin piece of skin stretched tight like a drum inside the ear; the eardrum vibrates when sound waves strike it

megaphone   instrument used to make the voice sound louder

nerve   thin fibre that carries messages between the brain and other parts of the body

pitch   how high or low a sound is

sound wave   wave or vibration that can be heard

vibrate   move back and forth quickly

Find out more
Books

All About Sound (All About Science), Angela Royston (Raintree, 2016)

Sound (Amazing Science), Sally Hewitt (Wayland, 2014)

Sound (Moving Up with Science), Peter Riley (Franklin Watts, 2015)

Websites

www.bbc.co.uk/bitesize/ks1/science/sounds_and_pitch/play/

This site has an interactive game about sounds and pitch.

www.bbc.co.uk/guides/z3wf34j

This site has lots of information about how sounds are made.

resources.woodlands-junior.kent.sch.uk/revision/science/sounds.html

This site has interactive games and activities about sound.

Comprehension questions

1. What happens to a sound wave when it hits a wall?

2. Explain what vibrations are.

3. If you blow strongly into a recorder, and then blow gently, do you think the sounds you make will be different?

Index